THE
BLACK UNICORN

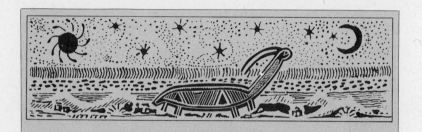

THE
BLACK UNICORN

POEMS BY AUDRE LORDE

W · W · NORTON & COMPANY · INC · NEW YORK

| ACKNOWLEDGMENTS

"Coniagui Women" first appeared in *The New Yorker* magazine. "Power" first appeared in the *Village Voice*, and is reprinted with permission.

Some of the other poems in this book have previously appeared in *Amazon Quarterly; The American Poetry Review; Aphra; Azalea; Black World; Chrysalis; Essence; First World; Freedomways: A Journal; Friendly Woman; Hudson River Anthology; The Iowa Review; The Massachusetts Review; Ms.; New York City Star; Nimrod; Poetry Now; Sinister Wisdom; Thirteenth Moon; Women: A Journal of Liberation.*

This book was completed with the assistance of a Creative Artist Public Service Award Grant.

BOOK DESIGN BY ANTONINA KRASS
TYPEFACES USED ARE V.I.P. PRIMER AND ABBOT OLD STYLE
MANUFACTURED BY VAIL-BALLOU PRESS, INC.

Library of Congress Cataloging in Publication Data
Lorde, Audre.
The black unicorn.
Bibliography: p.
I. Title.
PS3562.075B55   811'.5'4   78–17569
ISBN 0–393–04508–0
ISBN 0–393–04516–1 pbk.

1 2 3 4 5 6 7 8 9 0

FOR
LINDA GERTRUDE BELMAR LORDE

AND
FREDERICK BYRON LORDE

The Face Has Many Seasons

CONTENTS

I

II

III

IV

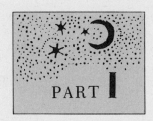

PART I

THE BLACK UNICORN

The black unicorn is greedy.
The black unicorn is impatient.
The black unicorn was mistaken
for a shadow
or symbol
and taken
through a cold country
where mist painted mockeries
of my fury.
It is not on her lap where the horn rests
but deep in her moonpit
growing.

The black unicorn is restless
the black unicorn is unrelenting
the black unicorn is not
free.

A WOMAN SPEAKS

Moon marked and touched by sun
my magic is unwritten
but when the sea turns back
it will leave my shape behind.
I seek no favor
untouched by blood
unrelenting as the curse of love
permanent as my errors
or my pride
I do not mix
love with pity
nor hate with scorn
and if you would know me
look into the entrails of Uranus
where the restless oceans pound.

I do not dwell
within my birth nor my divinities
who am ageless and half-grown
and still seeking
my sisters
witches in Dahomey
wear me inside their coiled cloths
as our mother did
mourning.

I have been woman
for a long time
beware my smile
I am treacherous with old magic
and the noon's new fury
with all your wide futures
promised
I am
woman
and not white.

FROM THE HOUSE OF YEMANJÁ

My mother had two faces and a frying pot
where she cooked up her daughters
into girls
before she fixed our dinner.
My mother had two faces
and a broken pot
where she hid out a perfect daughter
who was not me
I am the sun and moon and forever hungry
for her eyes.

I bear two women upon my back
one dark and rich and hidden
in the ivory hungers of the other
mother
pale as a witch
yet steady and familiar
brings me bread and terror
in my sleep
her breasts are huge exciting anchors
in the midnight storm.

All this has been
before
in my mother's bed
time has no sense
I have no brothers
and my sisters are cruel.

Mother I need
mother I need
mother I need your blackness now
as the august earth needs rain.

I am
the sun and moon and forever hungry
the sharpened edge
where day and night shall meet
and not be
one.

★ ★
*

CONIAGUI WOMEN

The Coniagui women
wear their flesh like war
bear children who have eight days
to choose their mothers
it is up to the children
who must decide to stay.

Boys burst from the raised loins
twisting and shouting
from the bush secret
they run
beating the other women
avoiding the sweet flesh
hidden
near their mother's fire
but they must take her blood as a token
the wild trees have warned them
beat her and you will be free
on the third day
they creep up to her cooking pot
bubbling over the evening's fire
and she feeds them
yam soup
and silence.

"Let us sleep in your bed" they whisper
"Let us sleep in your bed" they whisper
"Let us sleep in your bed"
but she has mothered before them.
She closes her door.

They become men.

A ROCK THROWN INTO THE
WATER DOES NOT FEAR THE COLD

In front of the City Hotel in Kumasi
two horned snails come at twilight
to eat the foot-long speckled snake
dead on an evening wall
from sudden violent storm.
Their white extended bodies
gently sucking
take sweetness from the stiffening shape
as darkness overtakes them.

9

★ ★
★

DAHOMEY

"in spite of the fire's heat
the tongs can fetch it."

It was in Abomey that I felt
the full blood of my fathers' wars
and where I found my mother
Seboulisa
standing with outstretched palms hip high
one breast eaten away by worms of sorrow
magic stones resting upon her fingers
dry as a cough.

In the dooryard of the brass workers
four women joined together dying cloth
mock Eshu's iron quiver
standing erect and flamingly familiar
in their dooryard
mute as a porcupine in a forest of lead
In the courtyard of the cloth workers
other brothers and nephews
are stitching bright tapestries
into tales of blood.

Thunder is a woman with braided hair
spelling the fas of Shango
asleep between sacred pythons
that cannot read
nor eat the ritual offerings
of the Asein.
My throat in the panther's lair
is unresisting.

Bearing two drums on my head I speak
whatever language is needed
to sharpen the knives of my tongue
the snake is aware although sleeping
under my blood
since I am a woman whether or not
you are against me
I will braid my hair
even
in the seasons of rain.

125TH STREET AND ABOMEY

Head bent, walking through snow
I see you Seboulisa
printed inside the back of my head
like marks of the newly wrapped akai
that kept my sleep fruitful in Dahomey
and I poured on the red earth in your honor
those ancient parts of me
most precious and least needed
my well-guarded past
the energy-eating secrets
I surrender to you as libation
mother, illuminate my offering
of old victories
over men over women over my selves
who has never before dared
to whistle into the night
take my fear of being alone
like my warrior sisters
who rode in defense of your queendom
disguised and apart
give me the woman strength
of tongue in this cold season.

Half earth and time splits us apart
like struck rock.
A piece lives elegant stories
too simply put
while a dream on the edge of summer
of brown rain in nim trees
snail shells from the dooryard
of King Toffah
bring me where my blood moves
Seboulisa mother goddess with one breast
eaten away by worms of sorrow and loss

see me now
your severed daughter
laughing our name into echo
all the world shall remember.

THE WOMEN OF DAN DANCE WITH
SWORDS IN THEIR HANDS TO MARK THE
TIME WHEN THEY WERE WARRIORS

I did not fall from the sky
I
nor descend like a plague of locusts
to drink color and strength from the earth
and I do not come like rain
as a tribute or symbol for earth's becoming
I come as a woman
dark and open
some times I fall like night
softly
and terrible
only when I must die
in order to rise again.

I do not come like a secret warrior
with an unsheathed sword in my mouth
hidden behind my tongue
slicing my throat to ribbons
of service with a smile
while the blood runs
down and out
through holes in the two sacred mounds
on my chest.

I come like a woman
who I am
spreading out through nights
laughter and promise
and dark heat
warming whatever I touch
that is living
consuming
only
what is already dead.

★ ★
*

SAHARA

High
above this desert
I am
becoming
absorbed.

Plateaus of sand
dendrites of sand
continents and islands and waddys
of sand
tongue sand
wrinkle sand
mountain sand
coasts of sand
pimples and pustules and macula of sand
snot all over your face from sneezing sand
dry lakes of sand
buried pools of sand
moon craters of sand
Get your "I've had too much of people"
out of here sand.

My own place sand
never another place sand
punishments of sand
hosannahs of sand
Epiphanies of sand
crevasses of sand
mother of sand
I've been here a long time sand
string sand
spaghetti sand
cat's cradle ring-a-levio sand
army of trees sand

jungle of sand
grief of sand
subterranean treasure sand
moonglade sand
male sand
terrifying sand

Will I never get out of here sand
open and closed sand
curvatures of sand
nipples of sand
hard erected bosoms of sand
clouds quick and heavy and
desperate sand
thick veil over my face sand
sun is my lover sand
footprints of the time on sand
navel sand
elbow sand
play hopscotch through the labyrinth sand
I have spread myself sand
I have grown harsh and flat
against you sand
glass sand
fire sand
malachite and gold diamond sand
cloisonné coal sand
filagree silver sand
granite and marble and ivory sand

Hey you come here and she came sand
I will endure sand
I will resist sand
I am tired of no
all the time sand
I too will unmask my dark
hard rock sand.

PART II

★ ★
★

HARRIET

Harriet there was always somebody calling us crazy
or mean or stuck-up or evil or black
or black
and we were
nappy girls quick as cuttlefish
scurrying for cover
trying to speak trying to speak
trying to speak
the pain in each others mouths
until we learned
on the edge of a lash
or a tongue
on the edge of the other's betrayal
that respect
meant keeping our distance
in silence
averting our eyes
from each other's face in the street
from the beautiful dark mouth
and cautious familiar eyes
passing alone.

I remember you Harriet
before we were broken apart
we dreamed the crossed swords
of warrior queens
while we avoided each other's eyes
and we learned to know lonely
as the earth learns to know dead
Harriet Harriet
what name shall we call our selves now
our mother is gone?

★ ⋆
⋆

CHAIN

News item: Two girls, fifteen and sixteen, were sent to foster homes,
because they had borne children by their natural father. Later,
they petitioned the New York courts to be returned to their
parents, who, the girls said, loved them. And the courts did so.

Faces surround me that have no smell or color no time
only strange laughing testaments
vomiting promise like love
but look at the skeleton children
advancing against us
beneath their faces there is no sunlight
no darkness
no heart remains
no legends
to bring them back as women
into their bodies at dawn.

Look at the skeleton children
advancing against us
we will find womanhood
in their eyes
as they cry
which of you bore me
will love me
will claim my blindness as yours
and which of you marches to battle
from between my legs?

II

On the porch outside my door
girls are lying
like felled maples in the path of my feet
I cannot step past them nor over them
their slim bodies roll like smooth tree trunks
repeating themselves over and over

until my porch is covered with the bodies
of young girls.
Some have a child in their arms.
To what death shall I look for comfort?
Which mirror to break or mourn?

Two girls repeat themselves in my doorway
their eyes are not stone.
Their flesh is not wood nor steel
but I can not touch them.
Shall I warn them of night
or offer them bread
or a song?
They are sisters. Their father has known
them over and over. The twins they carry
are his. Whose death shall we mourn
in the forest
unburied?
Winter has come and the children are dying.

One begs me to hold her between my breasts
Oh write me a poem mother
here, over my flesh
get your words upon me
as he got this child upon me
our father lover
thief in the night
do not be so angry with us. We told him
your bed was wider
but he said if we did it then
we would be his
good children if we did it
then he would love us
oh make us a poem mother
that will tell us his name
in your language
is he father or lover

we will leave your word
for our children
engraved on a whip or a golden scissors
to tell them the lies
of their birth.

Another says mother
I am holding your place.
Do you know me better than I knew him
or myself?
Am I his daughter or girlfriend
am I your child or your rival
you wish to be gone from his bed?
Here is your granddaughter mother
give us your blessing before I sleep
what other secrets
do you have to tell me
how do I learn to love her
as you have loved me?

SEQUELAE

Because a burning sword notches both of my doorposts
because I am standing between
my burned hands in the ashprint of two different houses
midnight finds weave a filigree of disorder
I figure in the dreams of people
who do not even know me
the night is a blister of stars
pierced by nightmares of a telephone ringing
my hand is the receiver
threatening as an uncaged motor
seductive as the pain of voiceless mornings
voiceless kitchens I remember
cornflakes shrieking like banshees in my throat
while I battle the shapes of you
wearing old ghosts of me
hating you for being
black and not woman
hating you for being white
and not me
in this carnival of memories
I name you both the laying down of power
the separation I cannot yet make
after all these years of blood
my eyes are glued
like fury to the keyholes
of yesterday
rooms
where I wander
solitary as a hunting cheetah
at play with legends call disaster
due all women who refuse to wait
in vain;

In a new room

25

I enter old places bearing your shape
trapped behind the sharp smell of your anger
in my voice
behind tempting invitations
to believe
your face
tipped like a pudding under glass
and I hear the high pitch of your voice
crawling out from my hearts
deepest culverts
compromise is a coffin nail
rusty as seaweed
tiding through an august house
where nobody lives
beyond choice
my pathways are strewn with old discontents
outgrown defenses still sturdy as firebrick
unlovely and dangerous as measles
they wither into uselessness
but do not decay.

Because I do not wish
to remember
but love to caress the deepest bone
of me
begging shes that wax and wane like moonfire
to absolve me at any price
I battle old ghosts of you
wearing the shapes of me
surrounded by black
and white faces
saying no over and over
becoming my mother draped in my fathers
bastard ambition
growing dark secrets
out from between her thighs
and night comes into me like a fever

my hands grip a flaming sword that screams
while an arrogant woman masquerading as a fish
plunges it deeper and deeper
into the heart we both share
like beggars
on this moment of time
where the space ships land
I have died too many deaths
that were not mine.

FOR ASSATA

New Brunswick Prison, 1977

In this new picture your smile has been to war
you are almost obscured by other faces
on the pages
those shadows are sisters
who have not yet spoken
your face is in shadow
obscured by the half-dark
by the thick bars running across your eyes
like sentinels
all the baby fat has been burned away
like a luxury your body let go
reluctantly
the corners of your mouth turn down
I cannot look into your eyes
who are all those others
behind you
the shadows are growing lighter
and more confusing.

I dream of your freedom
as my victory
and the victory of all dark women
who forego the vanities of silence
who war and weep
sometimes against our selves
in each other
rather than our enemies
falsehoods
Assata my sister warrior
Joan of Arc and Yaa Asantewa
embrace
at the back of your cell.

AT FIRST I THOUGHT
YOU WERE TALKING ABOUT...

Do you think I guess inasmuch as
so so
to be sure yes I see
what'd you mean
but listen yet and still on the other
hand like as if you know
oh
at first
I thought you were talking about
a bird a flower
your anguish
the precision of trial by fury
apes in the roses
a body-sized box
even my own mother's sadness
freezing into diamonds
sanctified beyond description
and brilliant as death.

There are 237 footfalls
from the parking lot
to this metal table
this mechanical desk of judgment
the early spring sun
shines
on the face of building
but is cut off at the door
now take my body and blood
as the last recorded sacrifice
of a negative image
upon the revolving doorpane
of this building
where even the elevators are tired

To be sure yes I know what did
you mean by the way
but listen yet and still on the other hand
like you know just as if
do you think I guess in as much as so-so
oh well I see
at first I thought you were talking
about . . .

A LITANY FOR SURVIVAL

For those of us who live at the shoreline
standing upon the constant edges of decision
crucial and alone
for those of us who cannot indulge
the passing dreams of choice
who love in doorways coming and going
in the hours between dawns
looking inward and outward
at once before and after
seeking a now that can breed
futures
like bread in our children's mouths
so their dreams will not reflect
the death of ours;

For those of us
who were imprinted with fear
like a faint line in the center of our foreheads
learning to be afraid with our mother's milk
for by this weapon
this illusion of some safety to be found
the heavy-footed hoped to silence us
For all of us
this instant and this triumph
We were never meant to survive.

And when the sun rises we are afraid
it might not remain
when the sun sets we are afraid
it might not rise in the morning
when our stomachs are full we are afraid
of indigestion
when our stomachs are empty we are afraid

we may never eat again
when we are loved we are afraid
love will vanish
when we are alone we are afraid
love will never return
and when we speak we are afraid
our words will not be heard
nor welcomed
but when we are silent
we are still afraid.

So it is better to speak
remembering
we were never meant to survive.

MEET

Woman when we met on the solstice
high over halfway between your world and mine
rimmed with full moon and no more excuses
your red hair burned my fingers as I spread you
tasting your ruff down to sweetness
and I forgot to tell you
I have heard you calling across this land
in my blood before meeting
and I greet you again
on the beaches in mines lying on platforms
in trees full of tail-tail birds flicking
and deep in your caverns of decomposed granite
even over my own laterite hills
after a long journey
licking your sons
while you wrinkle your nose at the stench.

Coming to rest
in the open mirrors of your demanded body
I will be black light as you lie against me
I will be heavy as August over your hair
our rivers flow from the same sea
and I promise to leave you again
full of amazement and our illuminations
dealt through the short tongues of color
or the taste of each other's skin as it hung
from our childhood mouths.

When we meet again
will you put your hands upon me
will I ride you over our lands
will we sleep beneath trees in the rain?
You shall get young as I lick your stomach
hot and at rest before we move off again

you will be white fury in my navel
I will be sweeping night
Mawulisa foretells our bodies
as our hands touch and learn
from each others hurt.
Taste my milk in the ditches of Chile and Ouagadougou
in Tema's bright port while the priestess of Larteh
protects us
in the high meat stalls of Palmyra and Abomey-Calavi
now you are my child and my mother
we have always been sisters in pain.

Come in the curve of the lion's bulging stomach
lie for a season out of the judging rain
we have mated we have cubbed
we have high time for work and another meeting
women exchanging blood
in the innermost rooms of moment
we must taste of each other's fruit
at least once
before we shall both be slain.

SEASONING

What am I ready to lose in this advancing summer?
As the days that seemed long
grow shorter and shorter
I want to chew up time
until every moment expands
in an emotional mathematic
tht includes the smell and texture
of every similar instant since I was born.

But the solstice is passing
my mouth stumbles
crammed with cribsheets and flowers
dimestore photographs
of loving in stages
choked by flinty nuggets of old friends
undigested enemies
preserved sweet and foul in their lack
of exposure to sunlight.
Thundereggs of myself
ossify in the buttonholes
of old recalled lovers
who all look like rainbows
stretching across other summers
to the pot of gold
behind my own eyes.

As the light wanes
I see
what I thought I was anxious to surrender
I am only willing to lend
and reluctance covers my face
as I glue up my lips with the promise
of coming winter.

TOURING

Coming in and out of cities
where I spend one or two days
selling myself
where I spend one or two nights
in beds that do not have the time to fit me
coming in and out of cities
too quickly
to be touched by their magic
I burn
from the beds that do not fit me
I leave sated
but without feeing
any texture of the house I have invaded
by invitation
I leave
with a disturbing sense
of the hard core of flesh
missed
and truly revealing.

I leave poems behind me
dropping them like dark seeds that
I will never harvest
that I will never mourn
if they are destroyed
they pay for a gift
I have not accepted.

Coming in and out of cities
untouched by their magic
I think without feeling
this is what men do
who try for some connection
and fail
and leave
five dollars on the table.

WALKING OUR BOUNDARIES

This first bright day has broken
the back of winter.
We rise from war
to walk across the earth
around our house
both stunned that sun can shine so brightly
after all our pain
Cautiously we inspect our joint holding.
A part of last year's garden still stands
bracken
one tough missed okra pod clings to the vine
a parody of fruit cold-hard and swollen
underfoot
one rotting shingle
is becoming loam.

I take your hand beside the compost heap
glad to be alive and still
with you
we talk of ordinary articles
with relief
while we peer upward
each half-afraid
there will be no tight buds started
on our ancient apple tree
so badly damaged by last winter's storm
knowing
it does not pay to cherish symbols
when the substance
lies so close at hand
waiting to be held
your hand
falls off the apple bark
like casual fire

along my back
my shoulders are dead leaves
waiting to be burned
to life.

The sun is watery warm
our voices
seem too loud for this small yard
too tentative for women
so in love
the siding has come loose in spots
our footsteps hold this place
together
as our place
our joint decisions make the possible
whole.
I do not know when
we shall laugh again
but next week
we will spade up another plot
for this spring's seeding.

EULOGY FOR ALVIN FROST

I.

Black men bleeding to death inside themselves
inside their fine strong bodies
inside their stomachs
inside their heads
a hole
as large as a dum-dum bullet
eaten away from the inside
death at 37.

Windows are holes to let in the light
in Newark airport at dawn I read
of your death by illumination
the carpets are dark and the windows are smoky
to keep out the coming sun
I plummet down through a hole in the carpet
seeking immediate ground for my feet to embrace
my toes have no wisdom no strength
to resist
they curl in a spasm of grief
of fury uprooted
It is dawn in the airport and nothing is open
I cannot even plant you a tree
the earth is still frozen
I write a card saying
machines grew the flowers I send
to throw into your grave.

On occasion we passed in the hallway
usually silent and hurried but fighting
on the same side.
You congratulate me on my latest book
in a Black Caucus meeting
you are distinguished
by your genuine laughter

and you might have been my long lost
second grade seat-mate named Alvin
grown into some other magic
but we never had time enough
just to talk.

II.

From an airplane heading south
the earth grows slowly greener
we pass the first swimming pool
filled with blue water
this winter is almost over
I don't want to write a natural poem
I want to write about the unnatural death
of a young man at 37
eating himself for courage in secret
until he vanished
bleeding to death inside.
He will be eulogized in echoes
by a ghost of those winters
that haunt morning people
wearing away our days like smiling water
in southern pools
leaving psychic graffiti
clogging the walls of our hearts
carving out ulcers inside our stomachs
from which we explode
or bleed to death.

III.

The day after your burial
John Wade slid off his chair
onto the carpet in the student cafeteria
and died there on the floor
between Abnormal Psychology and a half-finished

cup of black coffee.
Cafeteria guards rushed him out
the back door between classes
and we never knew until a week later
that he had even been ill.

I am tired of writing memorials to black men
whom I was on the brink of knowing
weary like fig trees
weighted like a crepe myrtle
with all the black substance poured into earth
before earth is ready to bear.
I am tired of holy deaths
of the ulcerous illuminations the cerebral accidents
the psychology of the oppressed
where mental health is the ability
to repress
knowledge of the world's cruelty.

IV.

Dear Danny who does not know me
I am
writing to you for your father
whom I barely knew
except at meetings where he was
distinguished
by his genuine laughter
and his kind bright words
Danny son of Alvin
please cry
whenever it hurts
remember to laugh
even when you do battle
stay away from coffee and fried plastic
even when it looks like chicken
and grow up

black and strong and beautiful
but not too soon.

We need you
and there are so few
left.

CHORUS

Sun
make me whole again
to love
the shattered truths of me
spilling out like dragon's teeth
through the hot lies
of those who say they love
me
when I am done
each shard will spring up
complete and armed
like a warrior woman
hot to be dealt with
slipping through alleyways
of musical night people humming
Mozart
was a white dude.

COPING

It has rained for five days
running
the world is
a round puddle
of sunless water
where small islands
are only beginning
to cope
a young boy
in my garden
is bailing out water
from his flower patch
when I ask him why
he tells me
young seeds that have not seen sun
forget
and drown easily.

TO MARTHA: A NEW YEAR

As you search over this year
with eyes your heart has
sharpened
remember longing.

I do not know your space now
I only seek a woman whom I love
trapped there
by accident.
but places do not change
so much
as what we seek in them
and faith will serve
along the way
to somewhere else
where work begins.

IN MARGARET'S GARDEN

When I first saw you blooming the color was now
protests sprang from your rapid hands
like a second set of fingers
you were learning to use
the betrayal of others
in place of your own pain
and your mouth was smiling
off-center
in the total confusion.

I never saw nor visited by day
the place where your swans
were conquered.
When I met you again
your mouth had centered
into aloneness
you said you had come apart
but your earth had been nourished
into a new garden of strong smells.

I felt you wanting
to mourn
the innocence of beginnings
that old desire for blandness.
I feel your sadness
deep in the center of me
and I make a pact with you sister
if you will not sorrow
I will not tell.

SCAR

This is a simple poem.
for the mothers sisters daughters
girls I have never been
for the women who clean the Staten Island ferry
for the sleek witches who burn
me at midnight
in effigy
because I eat at their tables
and sleep with their ghosts.

Those stones in my heart are you
of my own flesh
whittling me with your sharp false eyes
laughing me out of your skin
because you do not value your own
life
nor me.

This is a simple poem
I will have no mother no sister no daughter
when I am through
and only the bones are left
see how the bones are showing
the shape of us at war
clawing our own flesh out
to feed the backside of our masklike faces
that we have given the names of men.

Donald deFreeze I never knew you so well
as in the eyes of my own mirror
did you hope
for blessing or pardon
lying
in bed after bed

or was your eye sharp and merciless enough
to endure
beyond the deaths of wanting?

With your voice in my ears
with my voice in your ears
try to deny me
I will hunt you down
through the night veins of my own addiction
through all my unsatisfied childhoods
as this poem unfolds
like the leaves of a poppy
I have no sister no mother no children
left
only a tideless ocean of moonlit women
in all shades of loving
learning the dance of open and closing
learning a dance of electrical tenderness
no father no mother would teach them.

Come Sambo dance with me
pay the piper dangling dancing
his knee-high darling
over your wanting under your bloody
white faces come Bimbo come Ding Dong
watch the city falling down down
down lie down bitch slow down nigger
so you want a cozy womb to hide you
to pucker up and suck you back
safely
well I tell you what I'm gonna do
next time you head for the hatchet
really need some nook to hole up in
look me up
I'm the ticket taker on a queen
of roller coasters

I can get you off
cheap.

This is a simple poem
sharing my head with dreams
of a big black woman with jewels in her eyes
she dances
her head in a golden helmet
arrogant
plumed
her name in Colossa
her thighs are like stanchions
or flayed hickory trees
embraced in armour
she dances
slow earth-shaking motions
that suddenly alter
and lighten
as she whirls laughing
the tooled metal over her hips
comes to an end
and at the shiny edge
an astonishment
of soft black curly hair.

PORTRAIT

Strong women
know the taste
of their own hatred
I must always be
building nests
in a windy place
I want the safety of oblique numbers
that do not include me
a beautiful woman
with ugly moments
secret and patient
as the amused and ponderous elephants
catering to Hannibal's ambition
as they swayed on their own way
home.

A SONG FOR MANY MOVEMENTS

Nobody wants to die on the way
caught between ghosts of whiteness
and the real water
none of us wanted to leave
our bones
on the way to salvation
three planets to the left
a century of light years ago
our spices are separate and particular
but our skins sing in complimentary keys
at a quarter to eight mean time
we were telling the same stories
over and over and over.

Broken down gods survive
in the crevasses and mudpots
of every beleaguered city
where it is obvious
there are too many bodies
to cart to the ovens
or gallows
and our uses have become
more important than our silence
after the fall
too many empty cases
of blood to bury or burn
there will be no body left
to listen
and our labor
has become more important
than our silence.

Our labor has become
more important
than our silence.

BROTHER ALVIN

In the seat that we shared in the second grade
there was always a space between us
left for our guardian angels.
We had made it out of the brownies together
because you knew your numbers
and could find the right pages
while I could read all the words.
You were absent a lot between Halloween
and Thanksgiving
and just before Christmas vacation
you disappeared
along with the tinsel
and paper turkeys
and never returned.

My guardian angel and I had the seat to ourselves
for a little while only
until I was demoted back to the brownies
because I could never find the correct page.

You were not my first death.
but your going was not solaced by the usual
rituals of separation
the dark lugubrious murmurs
and invitations by threat
to the dignified grownups' view
of a child's inelegant pain
so even now
all these years of death later
I search through the index
of each new book
on magic
hoping to find some new spelling
of your name.

SCHOOL NOTE

My children play with skulls
for their classrooms are guarded by warlocks
who scream at the walls collapsing
into paper toilets
plump witches mouth ancient curses
in an untaught tongue
test children upon their meaning
assign grades
in a holocaust ranging
from fury down through contempt.

My children play with skulls
at school
they have already learned
to dream of dying
their playgrounds were graveyards
where nightmares of no
stand watch over rented earth
filled with the bones of tomorrow.

My children play with skulls
and remember
for the embattled
there is no place
that cannot be
home
nor is.

DIGGING

In the rusty pages of Gray's Anatomy
in witchcraft and chewing gum
on sundays
I have sought you in the rings around oak trees
on each of the twelve moons of Jupiter
on Harlem streets
peeping up at the secrets pregnant women carry
like a swollen threat
beneath the flowers of their gathered blouses
and under the breasts of a summer night
smelling of the kerosene and red pepper
my mother used to frighten out bedbugs
hidden between my toes
or was it only dream beads of sweat
I suffered
before I could slip
through nightmare
into the patient world of sleep
vanishing like a swallowed flower
and for years afterward I would wake
in August
to the left-over scent
of a child's tears
on my pillow.

In the stone machine
that smells of malachite and jasper
of coprolites undercutting and crazed
in the stone machine
twirled green dust burns my nose
like Whitsuntide fire.

I send you a gift of Malachite.
Of Amber, for melancholy.
Of Turquoise, for your heart's ease.

In the stone museum
ancient tapestries
underline sense
with an animal
touching the organ's place.

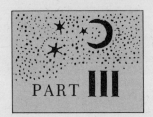

PART III

OUTSIDE

In the center of a harsh and spectrumed city
all things natural are strange.
I grew up in a genuine confusion
between grass and weeds and flowers
and what colored meant
except for clothes you couldn't bleach
and nobody called me nigger
until I was thirteen.
Nobody lynched my momma
but what she'd never been
had bleached her face of everything
but very private furies
and made the other children
call me yellow snot at school.

And how many times have I called myself back
through my bones confusion
black
like marrow meaning meat
and how many time have you cut me
and run in the streets
my own blood
who do you think me to be
that you are terrified of becoming
or what do you see in my face
you have not already discarded
in your own mirror
what face do you see in my eyes
that you will someday
come to
acknowledge your own?
Who shall I curse that I grew up
believing in my mother's face

or that I lived in fear of potent darkness
wearing my father's shape
they have both marked me
with their blind and terrible love
and I am lustful now for my own name.

Between the canyons of their mighty silences
mother bright and father brown
I seek my own shapes now
for they never spoke of me
except as theirs
and the pieces I stumble and fall over
I still record as proof
that I am beautiful
twice
blessed with the images
of who they were
and who I thought them once to be
of what I move
toward and through
and what I need
to leave behind me
most of all
I am blessed within my selves
who are come to make our shattered faces
whole.

THERAPY

Trying to see you
my eyes grow
confused
it is not your face
they are seeking
fingering through your spaces
like a hungry child
even now
I do not want
to make a poem
I want to make you
more and less
a part
from my self.

★ ★
*

THE SAME DEATH OVER AND OVER
OR
LULLABIES ARE FOR CHILDREN

"It's the small deaths in the supermarket" she said
trying to open my head
with her meat white cleaver
trying to tell me how
her pain met mine
halfway
between the smoking ruins in a black neighborhood of Los Angeles
and the bloody morning streets of child-killing New York.

Her poem reached like an arc across country and
"I'm trying to hear you" I said
roaring with my pain in a predawn city
where it is open season on black children
where my worst lullaby goes on over and over.
"I'm not fighting you" I said
"but it's the small deaths in the gutter
that are unmaking us all
and the white cop who shot down 10-year-old Clifford Glover
did not fire because he saw a girl.

BALLAD FOR ASHES

Nobody lives!
cried the thin man
high on the sunny stone steps
of my house
dreaming
he lied
I saw him come
flying
down to the ground
with a thud.

I touched his bruised face
with my fingers
in the low sun.

A man crept up
to a golden cup
to beg for a drink
the water was cold
but the edges of gold
slit his lips like a sieve.

A WOMAN/DIRGE
FOR WASTED CHILDREN

for Clifford

Awakening
rumors of the necessity for your death
are spread by persistent screaming flickers
in the morning light
I lie
knowing it is past time for sacrifice
I burn
like the hungry tongue of an ochre fire
like a benediction of fury
pushed before the heel of the hand
of the thunder goddess
parting earth's folds with a searching finger
I yield
one drop of blood
which I know instantly
is lost.

A man has had himself
appointed
legal guardian of fetuses.
Centuries of wasted children
warred and whored and slaughtered
anoint me guardian
for life.

But in the early light
another sacrifice is taken
unchallenged
a small dark shape rolls down
a hilly slope
dragging its trail of wasted blood
upon the ground
I am broken

into clefts of screaming
that sound like the drilling flickers
in treacherous morning air
on murderous sidewalks
I am bent
forever
wiping up blood
that should be
you.

PARTING

Belligerent and beautiful as a trapped ibis
your lean hands are a sacrifice
spoken three times
before dawn
there is blood in the morning egg
that makes me turn and weep
I see you
weaving pain into garlands
the shape of a noose
while I grow
weary
of licking my heart
for moisture
cactus tongued.

TIMEPIECE

In other destinies of choice
you could have come redheaded
with a star between your thighs
and morning like tender mushrooms
rising up around your toes
curled like a Shantung woman's toes
pausing to be loved
in the rice fields at noon
or as sharpened young eyeteeth
guarded in elegant blackness
erotic and hidden as yam shoots
in the parted mouth of dawn
balancing your craft as we went
upstream for water
Elegba's clay pot whistling upon your head.

But we were new for this time
and used wild-edged pieces of rock
struck off with a blunted hammer
spread
under high sun
and the rocks cry out
while we tell the course
of each other's tongue
with stones
in the place where the priestess
hurtled out palm-nuts
from enchanted fingers
and the stones mix
the colors of rainbows
flashing
you came like a wheaten song.

FOG REPORT

In this misty place where hunger finds us
seeking direction
I am too close to you to be useful.
When I speak
the smell of love on my breath
distracts you
and it is easier for me
to move
against myself in you
than to solve my own equations.

I am often misled
by your familiar comforts
the shape of your teeth is written
into my palm like a second lifeline
when I am fingerprinted
the taste of your thighs
shows up
outlined in the ink.
They found me wandering at the edge
of a cliff
beside nightmares of your body
"Give us your name and place of birth
and we will show you the way home."

I am tempted
to take you apart
and reconstruct your orifices
your tongue your truths your fleshy altars
into my own forgotten image
so when this fog lifts
I could be sure to find you
tethered like a goat
in my heart's yard.

PATHWAYS: FROM
MOTHER TO MOTHER

Tadpoles are legless and never learn to curtsy
birds cannot pee
in spring
black snakes go crazy
bowing out of the presence of kings.
Digging beneath a river bed
whose heart is black and rosy
I find the sticky ooze I learned
rejecting all my angels.
It puzzled my unborn children
and they paused in my frightened womb
a decade or two long
breaking apart what was begun
as marriage. My mother wept.
Fleshy lemmings dropped like corn
into her hopper
popping as they hit the water
and hungry tadpoles
winnowed up my falls.

Wherever she wore ivory
I wear pain.

Imprisoned in the pews of memory
beneath the scarlet velvet
is a smile. My mother
weeping
gouts of bloody wisdom
pewed oracular and seminal as rape
pursues me through the nightmares
of this wonderland of early learning
where I wander cryptic as a saint
tightmouthed as cuttlefish

darting beneath and over
vital flaws unstitched like crazy patchwork
until analyzed and useless I
crest in a shoal of missing mommies
paid and made in beds of consecration
worshiped by rituals in which
I do not believe
nor find a place to kneel and rest
out of the storm of strangers and demands
drowning in flooded churches
thick with rot and swollen with confusion
lashed to a raft of grins aligned in an enemy reason
I refuse to learn again.

Item: birds cannot pee
and so they shat upon our heads
while we learned how
to bow
out
of the presence of kings.

DEATH DANCE FOR A POET

Hidden in a forest of questions
unwilling to embrace blackthorn trees
to yield
to go into madness gracefully
or alone
the woman is no longer young
she has come to hate slowly
her skin of transparent metal
the sinuous exposure without reprieve
her eyes of clay
heavy with the fruit of prophetic dreaming.

In the hungers of silence
she has stolen her father's judgments
as the moon kneels
she lies
with her lover sun
wild with the pain
of her meticulous chemistry
her blind answers
the woman is eating her magic alone
crusts of quiet
breed a delusion
she is eternal
and stripping herself of night
she wanders
pretending
a borrowed fire
within her eyes.

Under the myrtle tree
unconcerned with not being
a birch
the woman with skin of transparent metal

lies on a cloak of sleep grass
closing at the first touch
unrelieved
clay-eyed and holy beyond comfort or mercy
she accepts the burden of sun
pouring a pan of burning salt
over her shining body
over the piercing revelations
of sinew and bone
her skin grows
soft and opaque.

And out of the ashes
and her range of vision
the executioners advance.

DREAM/SONGS FROM
THE MOON OF BEULAH LAND
I–V

I.

How much love can I pour into you I said
before it runs out of you
like undigested spinach
or shall I stuff you
like a ritual goose
with whatever you think
you want of me
and for whose killing
shall I grow you up
to leave me
to mourn
in the broken potsherds
upon my doorstep
in silent tears of the empty morning?

But I'm not going anywhere you said
why is there always
another question
beyond the last question
anuwered
out of your mouth
another storm?
It's happening
I said.

II.

Whenever I look for you the wind
howls with danger
beware the tree arms scream
what you are seeking
will find you
in the night
in the fist of your dreaming
and in my mouth
the words became sabers
cutting my boundaries
to ribbons
of merciless light.

III.

I dreamt you were driving me
in a big black Mazda
the car with a rotary engine
that ate up three kinds of gas at the same time
and whenever we came
to a station upon our journey
I would have to jump out
and explain
to the redfaced attendant
with a panting hose in his hand
that each kind of gas
gave us very different mileage
and we needed them all
for the combined use of all three
would get us to where we were going
with a great economy
of energy.

IV.

You say I am
sound as a drum
but that's very hard to be
as you cover your ears
with academic parchment
be careful
you might rip the cover
with your sharp nails
and then I will not sound at all.

To put us another way
what I come wrapped in
should be familiar to you
as hate is
what I come wrapped in
is close to you
as love is
close
to death
or your lying tongue
surveying the countries
of our mouths.

If I were drum
you would beat me
listening for the echo
of your own touch

not seeking
the voice of the spirit
inside the drum
only the spreading out shape
of your own hand on my skin
cover.

If I ever really sounded
I would rupture
your eardrums
or your heart.

V.

Learning to say goodbye
is finding a new tomorrow
on some cooler planet
barren and unfamiliar
and guiltless.

It costs the journey
to learn
letting go
of the burn-out rockets
to learn how
to light up space
with the quick fire of refusal
then drift gently down
to the dead surface
of the moon.

RECREATION

Coming together
it is easier to work
after our bodies
meet
paper and pen
neither care nor profit
whether we write or not
but as your body moves
under my hands
charged and waiting
we cut the leash
you create me against your thighs
hilly with images
moving through our word countries
my body
writes into your flesh
the poem
you make of me.

Touching you I catch midnight
as moon fires set in my throat
I love you flesh into blossom
I made you
and take you made
into me.

WOMAN

I dream of a place between your breasts
to build my house like a haven
where I plant crops
in your body —
an endless harvest
where the commonest rock
is moonstone and ebony opal
giving milk to all of my hungers
and your night comes down upon me
like a nurturing rain.

TIMING

In our infancy of action we were women of peace
come to service islands with no bridges in sight
in the beginning we all dreamed of an ending
but the wars of our childhood have aged us.

When donations of soup from my yesterday's kitchen
sour in the stomachs of beggars now miles away
and they toss in their sleep in doorways
with a curse of worry upon their lips
then even my good deeds are suspect
fulfillments of dreams of the dead
printing so many starvations
upon our future.
While we labor to feed the living
beware the spirit of the uneasy dead
who trap us into believing
in the too simple.

Our childhood wars have aged us
but it is the absence of change
which will destroy us
which has crippled our harvest into nightmare
of endless plowing through fields rank with death
while the carcasses of 4 million blackbirds
frozen to death because their chatter
insulted the generals
escape in the back pages
like the three black girls
hauled into an empty hurried courtroom
to point fingers at their mother—
I was cooking peasoup while they murmured—
"Yes, Mommy told us that she'd killed him
in front of many strangers she told us
yes he was a white man, may we go now?"

And their eyes look like old women who sleep
in the curve of neon doorways under newspaper
clutching a can of petfood for tomorrow's meal.

Sisters there is a hole in my heart
that is bearing your shapes
over and over
as I read only the headlines
of this morning's newspaper.

GHOST

Since I don't want to trip over your silence
over the gap that is you
in my dark
I will deal how it feels
with you
climbing another impossible mountain
with you gone
away a long time ago.

I don't want my life to be woven or chosen
from pain I am concealing
from fractions of myself
from your voice crying out in your sleep
to another woman
come play in the snow love
but this is not the same winter.

That was our first season of cold
I counted the patterned snowflakes
of love melting into ice
concealing our dreams of separation
I could not bear to write
our names on the mailbox
I could not bear to tell you my dreams
nor to question yours
now this poem
makes those mornings real again.

"You were always real" Bernice is saying
but I see the scars of her pain

hidden beneath the flesh on her cheekbones
and I do not know how many years I spent
trying to forget you
but I am afraid to think
how many years I will spend
trying to remember.

ARTISAN

In workshops without light
we have made birds
that do not sing
kites that shine
but cannot fly
with the speed
by which light falls
in the throat
of delicate working fire
I thought I had discovered
a survival kit
buried
in the moon's heart
flat and resilient as turtles
a case of tortoise shell
hung
in the mouth of darkness
precise unlikely markings
carved into the carapace
sweet meat beneath.

I did not recognize
the shape
of my own name.

Our bed spread
is a midnight flower
coming
all the way down
to the floor
there
your craft shows.

LETTER FOR JAN

No I don't think you were chicken not to speak
I think you
afraid I was mama as laser
seeking to eat out or change your substance
Mawulisa bent on destruction by threat
who might cover you
in a thick dark cloud of guilty symbols
smelling of sandalwood and old buffalo musk
of fiery offerings in the new moon's chalice
that would seduce you open
turning erotic and delightful as you
went under for the third time
your own poetry and sweetness
masked and drying out
upon your lips.

I do not even know
who looks like you
of all the sisters who come to me
at nightfall
we touch each other in secret places
draw old signs and stories
upon each other's back and proofread
each other's ancient copy.

You did not come to me speaking
because you feared
me as I might have been
god mother grown affluent
with the payment of old debts
or because you imaged me
as quick chic cutting
your praise song shared
to ribbons

thankless and separate as stormy gulfs
where lightning raged to pierce your clit
with proud black anger
or to reject you back into your doubt
smothering you into acceptance
with my own black song
coming over and over
as angry nightmares upon your pillow
to swallow you into confusion like a cherished berry
or buy you up at random with my electric body
shooting out rhythm and symbol
like lasers to burn you up and vanish
before the night.

When all the time
I would have loved you
speaking
being a woman full of loving
turned on
and a little bit raunchy
and heavy
with my own black song.

BICENTENNIAL POEM # 21,000,000

I know
the boundaries of my nation lie
within myself
but when I see old movies
of the final liberation of Paris
with french tanks rumbling over land
that is their own again
and old french men weeping
hats over their hearts
singing a triumphant national anthem

My eyes fill up with muddy tears
that have no earth to fall upon.

PART **IV**

THE OLD DAYS

Everyone wants to know
how it was in the old days
with no sun or moon in our colorless sky
to warn us we were not insane
only the harsh searing eye
of unblinking madwomen and men
calling our star a zoo
and I have no bride to recall
only many women who whisper
I was always a virgin
because I never remained.

I remember you only through the eyes
of all the forgotten others
on Monday a cat in the sorceresses' alley
screeched out your death
in another year's language
and I had forgotten
your name
like a promise of hunger.

Everyone wants to know how
it was
in the old days
when we kissed stone into dust
eternally hungry
paying respect to the crippled earth
in silence and in tears
surely one star fell as the mountain
collapsed over our bodies
surely the moon blinked once
as our vigils began.

CONTACT LENSES

Lacking what they want to see
makes my eyes hungry
and eyes can feel
only pain.

Once I lived behind thick walls
of glass
and my eyes belonged
to a different ethic
timidly rubbing the edges
of whatever turned them on.
Seeing usually
was a matter of what was
in front of my eyes
matching what was
behind my brain.
Now my eyes have become
a part of me exposed
quick risky and open
to all the same dangers.

I see much
better now
and my eyes hurt.

LIGHTLY

Don't make waves
is good advice
from a leaky boat.

One light year is the distance
one ray of light can travel in one year and
thirty
light years away from earth
in our infinitely offended universe
of waiting
an electronic cloud announces our presence
finally
to the unimpressable stars.

This is straight from a Scientific American
on the planet earth
our human signature upon the universe
is an elctronic cloud
of expanding 30-year-old television programs
like Howdy Doody Arthur Godfrey
Uncle Miltie and Hulahoops
quiz shows and wrestling midgets
baseball
the McCarthy hearings and Captain Kangaroo.

Now I don't know what
a conscious universe might be
but it is interesting to wonder
what will wave back
to all that.

HANGING FIRE

I am fourteen
and my skin has betrayed me
the boy I cannot live without
still sucks his thumb
in secret
how come my knees are
always so ashy
what if I die
before morning
and momma's in the bedroom
with the door closed.

I have to learn how to dance
in time for the next party
my room is too small for me
suppose I die before graduation
they will sing sad melodies
but finally
tell the truth about me
There is nothing I want to do
and too much
that has to be done
and momma's in the bedroom
with the door closed.

Nobody even stops to think
about my side of it
I should have been on Math Team
my marks were better than his
why do I have to be
the one
wearing braces
I have nothing to wear tomorrow

will I live long enough
to grow up
and momma's in the bedroom
with the door closed.

BUT WHAT CAN YOU
TEACH MY DAUGHTER

What do you mean
no no no no
you don't have the right
to know
how often
have we built each other
as shelters
against the cold
and even my daughter knows
what you know
can hurt you
she says her nos
and it hurts
she says
when she talks of liberation
she means freedom
from that pain
she knows
what you know
can hurt
but what you do
not know
can kill.

FROM INSIDE AN EMPTY PURSE

Money cannot buy you
what you want
standing flatfooted
and lying
like a grounded chestnut
unlovable and suspect
I am trying to reach
you
on whatever levels
you flow from
treacherous growing
water
in a blind tongueless pond.

I am the thread of your woman's cloth
the sexy prison that protects you
deep and unspoken
flesh around your freedom
I am your enemy's face.

The money doesn't matter
so much
as the lie
telling
you don't know
why
in a dream
I am trying to reach
you before
you fall in
to me.

A SMALL SLAUGHTER

Day breaks without thanks or caution
past a night without satisfaction or pain.
My words are blind children I have armed
against the casual insolence of morning
without you
I am scarred and marketed
like a streetcorner in Harlem
a woman
whose face in the tiles
your feet have not yet regarded
I am the stream
past which you will never step
the woman you can not deal with
I am the mouth
of your scorn.

FROM THE GREENHOUSE

Summer rains like my blood cries
lover my lover
over and over surging receding sometimes
a brief sun knifing through
rain like my blood speaks
in alternate whispers
roaring giving and taking seeking destroying
beseeching green sprouts
in our struggling garden
blessing the earth as it suffers
blind rain beating down
tender sprouts
in the silent mud.

My blood yells against
your sleeping shoulder
this is a poem of summer
my blood screams at your false safety
your mute body beside me
driving me closer and closer
you seek your own refuge
farther and farther away
in your dreaming
the edge of our bed is approaching
again
rain surges against our windows
green sprouts are drowning
in mud and blessings
in our carefully planted greenhouse
I have moved as far as I can
now my blood merges
into your dreaming.

★ ★
★

JOURNEYSTONES
I–XI

I.

Maxine
I used to admire your talent
for saying nothing
so well
that way the blood
was always someone else's
and there was always
someplace left
to be yourself
the stranger.

II.

Elaine
my sister outsider
I still salute
the power of learning
loss.

III.

China
girl on the run
I am sorry
our night
was not black enough
for you
to hide in.

IV.

Jan
was a name
for so many people
I cannot remember
you.

V.

Margaret
the broken rock you dropped
into my pocket
had unrelenting curves
that would not polish.
I discovered
it was the petrified half-shell
of a prehistoric nut.

VI.

Catherine
you lie
against the earth
like a little pungent onion
and whenever I come
too close to you
I weep.

VII.

Isabel
I hear your blood ring
but I am tired
of friends who hurt
and lean
at the same time

my heart grows
confused
between your need for love
and your need for destruction.

VIII.

Joyce
you always hated
being furious
and without anyone
to kill.

IX.

Janie
I feel the scream
drowning in your sharp eyes
trained to impersonate mermaids
shallow seductive
and dangerous as coral.

X.

Flora my sister
what I know
I no longer need
to understand.

If you make me stone
I will bruise you.

XI.

The last hole in fortune
is the anger of the empress
knowing herself as mortal
and without child.

ABOUT RELIGION

After church
on Sundays
I learned to love
the gospel music
swelling up past garbage cans in the summer
backyards of my childhood armageddon.

Black shiny women
spicy as rocking pumpkins
encased in stiff white covers
long sleeved
silk against brick
and their rocketed beat
snapped like pea shooters
in the august time
while the fingered tambourines
hand heeled beat
rose through the air shafts
sweet and timely.

I hear the music filtered
through a heat wave
of my mother's churchly disapproval.
A skinny nappy-headed little girl
ran back and forth collecting
in my envy
coins wrapped in newspapers
and the corners of old sheets
that even my mother
grudgingly
flung down.

SISTER OUTSIDER

We were born in a poor time
never touching
each other's hunger
never
sharing our crusts
in fear
the bread became enemy.

Now we raise our children
to respect themselves
as well as each other.

Now you have made loneliness
holy and useful
and no longer needed
now
your light shines very brightly
but I want you
to know
your darkness also
rich
and beyond fear.

BAZAAR

The lay back women are cooking
gold in their iron pots
is smoking
toward a sky that will never speak
in this evening I hold them
bound in the skin of my mother
anxious and ugly as a lump of iron
wishing to be worked for gold
other forgotten faces
of her
flow into each other
over the clatter
of remembered bargains
reluctant barter
I wonder
how many of these women (my sisters)
still have milk in their breasts.

* ★ ·
*

POWER

The difference between poetry and rhetoric
is being
ready to kill
yourself
instead of your children.

I am trapped on a desert of raw gunshot wounds
and a dead child dragging his shattered black
face off the edge of my sleep
blood from his punctured cheeks and shoulders
is the only liquid for miles and my stomach
churns at the imagined taste while
my mouth splits into dry lips
without loyalty or reason
thirsting for the wetness of his blood
as it sinks into the whiteness
of the desert where I am lost
without imagery or magic
trying to make power out of hatred and destruction
trying to heal my dying son with kisses
only the sun will bleach his bones quicker.

The policeman who shot down a 10-year-old in Queens
stood over the boy with his cop shoes in childish blood
and a voice said "Die you little motherfucker" and
there are tapes to prove that. At his trial
this policeman said in his own defense
"I didn't notice the size or nothing else
only the color." and
there are tapes to prove that, too.

Today that 37-year-old white man with 13 years of police forcing
has been set free
by 11 white men who said they were satisfied

justice had been done
and one black woman who said
"They convinced me" meaning
they had dragged her 4' 10" black woman's frame
over the hot coals of four centuries of white male approval
until she let go the first real power she ever had
and lined her own womb with cement
to make a graveyard for our children.

I have not been able to touch the destruction within me.
But unless I learn to use
the difference between poetry and rhetoric
my power too will run corrupt as poisonous mold
or lie limp and useless as an unconnected wire
and one day I will take my teenaged plug
and connect it to the nearest socket
raping an 85-year-old white woman
who is somebody's mother
and as I beat her senseless and set a torch to her bed
a greek chorus will be singing in 3/4 time
"Poor thing. She never hurt a soul. What beasts they are."

EULOGY

A girl in my sister's house
wears nightmare
hidden in her eyes
still as a bird's eyes.
When blood calls
the girl retreats into a brassy ring
that neither tears nor nourishment
can alter.

But a circle does not suffer
nor can it dream.
Her fingers twist into a married root
night cannot break her now
nor the sun heal
and soon its merciless white heat
will fuse
her nightmare eyes
to agate
her sullen tongue
to flint.

Then she will strike
but never bleed again.

"NEVER TAKE FIRE
FROM A WOMAN"

My sister and I
have been raised to hate
genteelly
each other's silences
sear up our tongues
like flame
we greet each other
with respect
meaning
from a watchful distance
while we dream of lying
in the tender of passion
to drink from a woman
who smells like love.

★ *
 *

BETWEEN OURSELVES

Once when I walked into a room
my eyes would seek out the one or two black faces
for contact or reassurance or a sign
I was not alone
now walking into rooms full of black faces
that would destroy me for any difference
where shall my eyes look?
Once it was easy to know
who were my people.

If we were stripped to our strength
of all pretense
and our flesh was cut away
the sun would bleach all our bones as white
as the face of my black mother
was bleached white by gold
or Orishala
and how
does that measure me?

I do not believe
our wants have made all our lies
holy.

Under the sun on the shores of Elmina
a black man sold the woman who carried
my grandmother in her belly
he was paid with bright yellow coin
that shone in the evening sun
and in the faces of her sons and daughters.
When I see that brother behind my eyes
his irises are bloodless and without color
his tongue clicks like yellow coins
tossed up on this shore

where we share the same corner
of an alien and corrupted heaven
and whenever I try to eat
the words
of easy blackness as salvation
I taste the color
of my grandmother's first betrayal.

I do not believe
our wants
have made all our lies
holy.

But I do not whistle his name at the shrine of Shopona
I do not bring down the rosy juices of death upon him
nor forget Orishala
is called the god of whiteness
who works in the dark wombs of night
forming the shapes we all wear
so that even cripples and dwarfs and albinos
are scared worshipers
when the boiled corn is offered.

Humility lies
in the face of history
I have forgiven myself
for him
for the white meat
we all consumed in secret
before we were born
we shared the same meal.
When you impale me
upon your lances of narrow blackness
before you hear my heart speak
mourn your own borrowed blood
your own borrowed visions.
Do not mistake my flesh for the enemy

do not write my name in the dust
before the shrine of the god of smallpox
for we are all children of Eshu
god of chance and the unpredictable
and we each wear many changes
inside of our skin.

Armed with scars
healed
in many different colors
I look in my own faces
as Eshu's daughter crying
if we do not stop killing
the other
in ourselves
the self that we hate
in others
soon we shall all lie
in the same direction
and Eshidale's priests will be very busy
they who alone can bury
all those who seek their own death
by jumping up from the ground
and landing upon their heads.

FUTURE PROMISE

This house will not stand forever.
The windows are sturdy
but shuttered
like individual solutions
that match one at a time.

The roof leaks.
On persistent rainy days
I look up to see
the gables weeping
quietly.

The stairs are sound
beneath my children
but from time to time
a splinter leaves
imbedded in a childish foot.

I dream of stairways
sagging
into silence
well used and satisfied
with no more need
for changelessness

Once
freed from constancy
this house
will not stand
forever.

THE TROLLOP MAIDEN

But my life is not portable now
said the trollop maiden
I need fixed light
to make my witless orchids
grow
into prizes
and the machine I use
to make my bread
is too bulky to move around
easily and besides
it needs
especially heavy current.

But the old maid who lives in your navel
is the trollop maiden's desire
and your orchids sing without smell
in the fixed light like sirens.

You can always run off
yourself
said the trollop maiden
but my life is not portable
yet she moved
into coquette with the rhythms
of a gypsy fiddle—
fired across my bow
with a mouthful of leaden pain
NOW
That's one piece I cannot leave behind
she whispered.

SOLSTICE

We forgot to water the plantain shoots
when our houses were full of borrowed meat
and our stomachs with the gift of strangers
who laugh now as they pass us
because our land is barren
the farms are choked with stunted rows of straw
and with our nightmares
of juicy brown yams that cannot fill us.
The roofs of our houses rot from last winter's water
but our drinking pots are broken
we have used them to mourn the deaths of old lovers
the next rain will wash our footprints away
and our children have married beneath them.

Our skins are empty.
They have been vacated by the spirits
who are angered by our reluctance
to feed them.
In baskets of straw made from sleep grass
and the droppings of civets
they have been hidden away by our mothers
who are waiting for us by the river.

My skin is tightening
soon I shall shed it
like a monitor lizard
like remembered comfort
at the new moon's rising
I will eat the last signs of my weakness
remove the scars of old childhood wars
and dare to enter the forest whistling
like a snake that has fed the chameleon
for changes
I shall be forever.

May I never remember reasons
for my spirit's safety
may I never forget
the warning of my woman's flesh
weeping at the new moon
may I never lose
that terror
that keeps me brave
May I owe nothing
that I cannot repay.

A GLOSSARY OF AFRICAN
NAMES USED IN THE POEMS

ABOMEY: The inland capital and heart of the ancient kingdom of Daho-
mey. A center of culture and power, it was also the seat of the courts of
the Aladaxonu, the famed Panther Kings.

AKAI: Tight narrow braids of hair wrapped with thread and arranged
about the head to form the elaborate coiffure of modern Dahomean high
fashion.

AMAZONS: Unlike in other African systems of belief, women in Daho-
mey, as the Creators of Life, were not enjoined from the shedding of
blood. The Amazons were highly prized, well-trained, and ferocious
women warriors who guarded, and fought under the direction of, the
Panther Kings of Dahomey.

ASEIN: Small metal altars upon high poles before which the deified an-
cestors are worshiped with offerings.

CONIAQUI: A West African people who occupy the area which is now
part of Guinea and the Ivory Coast.

DAN: An ancient name for the kingdom of Dahomey (Danhomee).

ELEGBA, ELEGBARA, LEGBA: See ESHU.

ESHIDALE: A local *Orisha* of the Ife region in Nigeria, whose priests
atone for and bury those who commit suicide by jumping up from the
ground and falling upon their heads.

ESHU: Also known as Elegba in Dahomey and the New World, Eshu is
the youngest and most clever son of Yemanjá (or of Mawulisa). The
mischievous messenger between all the other *Orisha-Vodu* and hu-
mans, he knows their different languages and is an accomplished
linguist who both transmits and interprets. This function is of para-
mount importance because the *Orisha* do not understand each other's
language, nor the language of humans. Eshu is a prankster, also, a per-
sonification of all the unpredictable elements in life. He is often iden-
tified with the masculine principle, and his primary symbol is frequently

a huge erect phallus. But Eshu-Elegba has no priests, and in many Dahomean religious rituals, his part is danced by a woman with an attached phallus. Because of his unpredictable nature, Eshu's shrines are built outside of every dwelling and village, and near every crossroads. He receives the first portion of any offering made to any other *Orisha-Vodu*, to help insure correct transmittal and a speedy answer.

FA: One's personal destiny—the personification of fate. This is also the name given to a widespread and elaborate metaphysical system of divination much used in Dahomey. Fa is sometimes called the writing of Mawulisa.

MAWULISA: Within the major pantheon of the *Vodu*, Mawulisa is the Dahomean female-male, sky-goddess-god principle. Sometimes called the first inseparable twins of the Creator of the Universe, Mawulisa (Mawu-Lisa) is also represented as west-east, night-day, moon-sun. More frequently, Mawu is regarded as the Creator of the Universe, and Lisa is either called her first son, or her twin brother. She is called the mother of all the other *Vodu*, and as such, is connected to the *Orisha* Yemanja. (See also: SEBOULISA.)

ORISHA: The *Orisha* are the goddesses and gods—divine personifications—of the Yoruba peoples of Western Nigeria. As the Yoruba were originally a group of many different peoples with a similar language, there are close to six hundred *Orisha*, major and local, with greater or lesser powers, some overlapping.

The neighboring people of Dan, or Dahomey, as it came to be called, received many of their religious forms from the Yoruba, so many of the *Orisha* reappear with different names as Dahomean goddesses and gods, or *Vodu* (*Vodun*). These *Orisha* frequently became the chief *Vodu* of a group of other natively Dahomean divine principles having similar powers and interests.

The *Orisha-Vodu* are divine, but not omnipotent. They are very powerful, but not always just. They are very involved in human affairs, and offerings must be made to maintain their good wishes. Many of the names and rituals of the *Orisha-Vodu* survive and flourish in religions practiced in Cuba, Brazil, Haiti, Grenada, and the United States. It is in Haiti and the U.S. that the religious traditions of Yoruba and Dahomey are most closely blended.

ORISHALA: A major *Orisha,* Orishala gives shape and form to humans in the womb before birth. His priests are in charge of burying women who die in pregnancy. He is sometimes also called Obatala, which means the God of Whiteness. (In the New World religions, Obatala is frequently female.) Those who are born crippled or deformed are under Orishala's special protection. Some say these cripples and albinos were made purposely by the *Orisha* so that his worship would not be forgotten; others say that those deformed were errors fashioned during Orishala's drunkenness. Red palm oil and wine are taboo at his shrine, and the color white is sacred to him, as are all white foods.

SHANGO: One of Yemanjá's best-known and strongest sons, Shango is the *Orisha* of lightning and thunder, war, and politics. His colors are bright red and white, and his symbol is a two-headed axe. In Nigeria, the head of the Shango cult is frequently a woman, called the Alagba. In Dahomey, he is known as Hervioso, chief *Vodu* of the Thunder Pantheon.

SHOPONA: The *Orisha* of smallpox. He is the god of earth and growing things; the disease is considered the most severe punishment for those who break his taboos, or whose names are whistled near his shrine. Lesser punishments are measles and boils and other skin eruptions. He is very powerful and greatly feared. In Dahomey, he is called Sagbatá, and long before Jenner in Europe, Sagbatá's priests knew and practiced the principle of live vaccination, guarding it jealously.

SEBOULISA: The goddess of Abomey—"The Mother of us all." A local representation of Mawulisa, she is sometimes known as Sogbo, creator of the world. (See also: MAWULISA.)

YAA ASANTEWA: An Ashanti Queen Mother in what is now Ghana, who led her people in several successful wars against the British in the nineteenth century.

YEMANJÁ: Mother of the other *Orisha,* Yemanjá is also the goddess of oceans. Rivers are said to flow from her breasts. One legend has it that a son tried to rape her. She fled until she collapsed, and from her breasts, the rivers flowed. Another legend says that a husband insulted Yemanjá's long breasts, and when she fled with her pots he knocked her down. From her breasts flowed the rivers, and from her body then sprang forth all the other *Orisha*. River-smooth stones are Yemanjá's symbol, and the sea is sacred to her followers. Those who please her are blessed with many children.

BIBLIOGRAPHY

Bascom, William. *The Yoruba of Southwestern Nigeria*. Holt, Rinehart & Winston. New York. 1969.

Courlander, Harold. *Tales of Yoruba Gods and Heroes*. Fawcett. Greenwich, Conn. 1973.

Herskovits, Melville. *Dahomey, Vols. I & II*. J. J. Augustin. New York. 1934.

Yoruba Temple. *The Gods of Africa*. Great Benin Books. New York. n.d.